For Lirit and Bennett. I love you so much!

Thanks to Sharon Schanzer for voluntarily guiding the publication of this book.
Thanks to Susan Korman for copy-editing.
Hugs to all our family and friends whose love and support sustained me on this journey.

www.mommyscancer.org   First Edition, September 2010

ISBN: 978-1-4520-7447-4 (sc)

First published by AuthorHouse 11/22/2010

AuthorHouse™
1663 Liberty Drive
Bloomington, IN 47403
www.authorhouse.com
Phone: 1-800-839-8640

Printed in the United States of America
This book is printed on acid-free paper.

This is Daddy, Mommy, Lirit, and Bennett. It reminds me of Mommy.

Bennett Miller, 3 ½ years old

In Memory
of
Ellen Meyer
Miller

Generous gifts to

The

Library
FOUNDATION

further the work of Multnomah County Library

Mommy's Cancer

Ellen R. Meyer

~

Illustrations by

Emelia BensonMeyer

When Lirit was a little girl and Bennett was a tiny baby they lived with Mommy and Daddy in a peach-colored house in Portland, Oregon. The house had pretty flowers in front and back. It was near friends, a park, and many stores.

Their family was happy and had lots of fun together. They liked to take walks and hikes together. They liked to play in the house and at the park together. They liked to sing and dance together. They liked to have parties and celebrations together.

One day Mommy became very sick. She could not take walks or go to the park. She could not drive. She could not cook dinner. What Mommy wanted most was to take care of Lirit and Bennett and to play with them. But she did not have enough energy. Instead, she had to lie in bed.

When Aunt Carolyn heard that Mommy was sick, she said, "I will take an airplane to Portland. I want to help." Lirit and Bennett were excited to see Aunt Carolyn. But they were sad that Mommy was sick.

Daddy and Mommy met with lots of doctors to help Mommy feel better. Mommy kept getting sicker. Finally, she went to the hospital.

Daddy, Lirit, Bennett, and Aunt Carolyn visited Mommy. She had lots of tubes coming out of her mouth and her arms. Lirit said, "You look scary, Mommy." Bennett was frightened. But Mommy was still Mommy. Lirit and Bennett gave her lots of snuggles and hugs. That helped them all feel better.

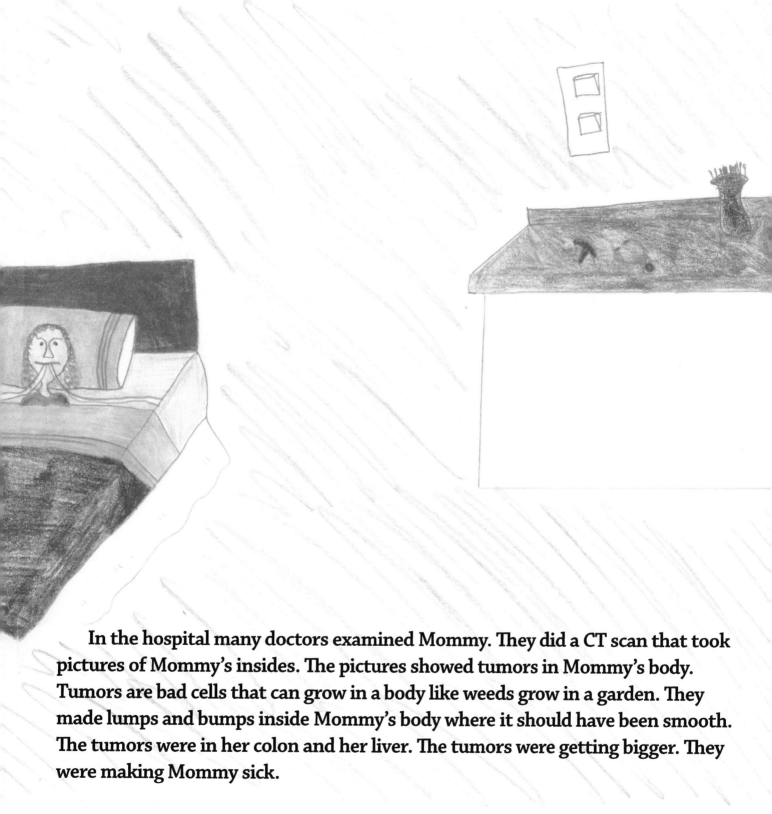

In the hospital many doctors examined Mommy. They did a CT scan that took pictures of Mommy's insides. The pictures showed tumors in Mommy's body. Tumors are bad cells that can grow in a body like weeds grow in a garden. They made lumps and bumps inside Mommy's body where it should have been smooth. The tumors were in her colon and her liver. The tumors were getting bigger. They were making Mommy sick.

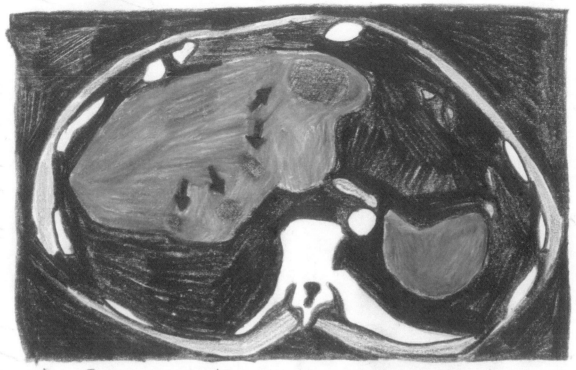

A CT scan that shows a picture of the tumors from colon cancer that were inside Mommy's body.

The doctors performed surgery to take the tumors out. They were able to take out some of the lumps and bumps, but not all of them. The doctors explained that Mommy's tumors were from a sickness called colon cancer.

Mommy stayed in the hospital for ten days. It seemed like a long time to Lirit and Bennett. Lirit asked over and over, "When will Mommy come home?" It felt like a long time to Mommy and Daddy, too. Mommy missed being at home with her family.

Finally, the doctor said, "Mommy is strong enough to leave the hospital."
Mommy, Daddy, Lirit, and Bennett were happy they would be home together again.

Mommy and Daddy told Lirit and Bennett about Mommy's cancer. "Cancer isn't anybody's fault," explained Mommy. "No one knows why I have cancer. But we do know that no one can get cancer from another person. It is not like catching a cold or the flu."

Then Mommy made a special promise to Lirit and Bennett. "I will do everything I can to fight the cancer. I want to be healthy to play with you and to take care of you. I love you so much."

O = Chemo Medicine

The doctors helped Mommy and Daddy make a plan to fight the cancer. Mommy would go to the clinic every Wednesday to get chemo medicine. She would also take chemo medicine home in a pump inside her purse. It would pump medicine into her body for two extra days.

Chemo medicine is very powerful. It has to be strong and powerful to fight cancer! Unfortunately, it also made Mommy tired. When she came home from getting chemo medicine, sometimes Mommy rested if she was too tired to play with Lirit and Bennett. The chemo medicine also gave her a red, bumpy rash on her face and made her hair fall out. These things made Mommy look different. But she was still Mommy. "Mommy, I think you look beautiful!" Lirit said.

Every Wednesday, Daddy brought Mommy to the clinic for more medicine. Sometimes Lirit or Bennett would go, too. They visited the big clinic building and looked through all the windows. There was a lot to see! They could see bridges, cars, buildings, and the river. They especially liked to watch the tram that went up and down a hill.

PORTLAND

ARCATA

SAN FRANCISCO

SALT LAKE CITY

LOS ANGELES

PHOENIX

CHICAGO

While Mommy was fighting cancer, lots of family came from far away to visit. Lirit and Bennett had fun when their grandparents, uncles, aunts, and cousins stayed at their house.

NEW YORK

WASHINGTON D.C.

Many friends came to visit, too. They came from San Francisco, New York, Chicago, Salt Lake, and Washington DC. Friends from Portland visited, too. Lirit and Bennett learned that family and friends from far and near loved them very much.

Lirit and Bennett went to a cancer counselor to play and to talk about their feelings about cancer. Before each appointment, Lirit would ask, "Can we play with the dollhouse and the doctor equipment?" Mommy always answered, "Yes!" Lirit and Bennett enjoyed these meetings.

Once the whole family flew on an airplane to Texas to fight Mommy's cancer. In Texas there is a special clinic and a big hospital with expert doctors to help people with cancer.

The family stayed near the hospital. Grandma, Grandpa, Aunt Carolyn, Uncle John, Uncle Chuck, and friends came, too. Lirit and Bennett visited lots of parks, museums and restaurants. They had fun, but they were sad that Mommy was still sick.

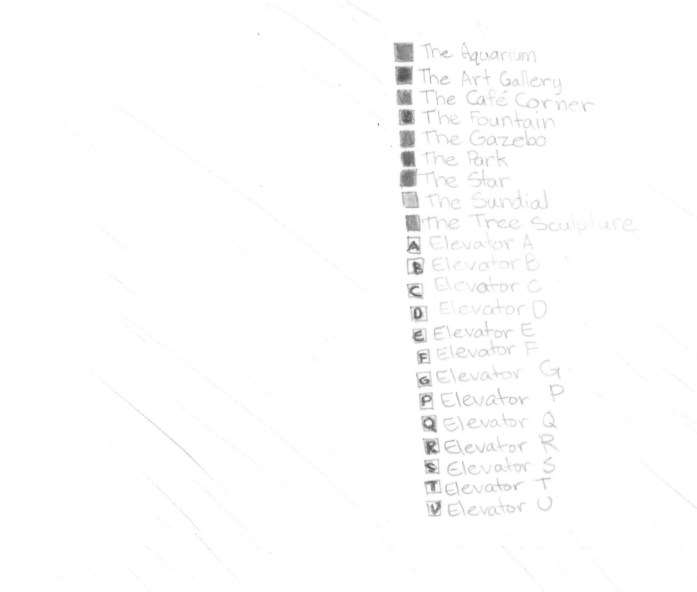

The Aquarium
The Art Gallery
The Café Corner
The Fountain
The Gazebo
The Park
The Star
The Sundial
The Tree Sculpture
A Elevator A
B Elevator B
C Elevator C
D Elevator D
E Elevator E
F Elevator F
G Elevator G
P Elevator P
Q Elevator Q
R Elevator R
S Elevator S
T Elevator T
U Elevator U

At the hospital, the doctors tried to cut the rest of the tumors out of Mommy's body. Unfortunately, they could not get them all out.

MAP OF HOSPITAL

After surgery Mommy stayed in the hospital for a week. Then she stayed at the apartment in Texas with Lirit, Bennett and Daddy. Finally, the whole family flew home to Portland together. While Mommy's body was recovering from surgery, she did not take chemo medicine.

For a long time after surgery Mommy was not able to lift Lirit or Bennett. Lirit and Bennett were sad that Mommy could not carry them. But Bennett and Mommy learned how to bump down the stairs together. Bennett giggled as they bumped down. He and Mommy had fun!

Slowly Mommy grew stronger and stronger. At last she could lift Lirit and Bennett! "Hooray!" Lirit cheered. Bennett smiled and laughed.

Soon it was time for Mommy to take chemo medicine again. Every two weeks, while Lirit went to pre-school and Bennett played with Nanny Debbie, Mommy went to the clinic.

Sometimes the chemo medicine made Mommy feel tired or sick. And sometimes it made her feel cranky. When she felt tired or cranky, she yelled at Lirit or Bennett even though she didn't want to. Lirit and Bennett did not like it when Mommy yelled!

After she yelled, Mommy always said, "I'm sorry. Sometimes the chemo medicine makes me do things I shouldn't do." Lirit and Bennett always forgave her.

Most days Mommy felt good. On these days, Lirit and Bennett's family did things like before Mommy had cancer. They played together in their peach-colored house. They read stories together. They ate together. They danced together. They went to the park together. They went to music and gymnastics classes together. They took fun vacations together. And they laughed together. Lots of times Lirit and Bennett did not think about Mommy's cancer.

Mommy continued to fight the cancer with chemo medicine for a long, long time. Sometimes Lirit and Bennett worried about Mommy's cancer. So did Mommy, Daddy, and their family and friends. But Mommy fought the cancer so that she could play with Lirit and Bennett and take care of them.

Mommy did this because she loved Lirit, Bennett, and Daddy SO MUCH! And Mommy knew that Lirit, Bennett, and Daddy loved her, too.

We were happy to see all the visitors. But we were sad because Mommy's cancer was not going away.

Lirit Miller, 6 years old

CPSIA information can be obtained
at www.ICGtesting.com
234321LV00001B